MW01146409

# THE
# RIDDLE
## OF THE
# TONGUE-
# STONES

Published by Word on Fire Votive, an imprint of
Word on Fire, Elk Grove Village, IL 60007
© 2024 by Word on Fire Catholic Ministries
Printed in Italy
All rights reserved

Cover design and typesetting by Nicolas Fredrickson

Interior art direction by Nicolas Fredrickson, Rozann Lee, and Haley Stewart

Scientific review by Kelly Kindstrom, PhD

Editing by Haley Stewart

Copyediting by James O'Neil

No part of this book may be used or reproduced in any manner whatsoever
without written permission, except in the case of brief quotations in critical
articles or reviews. For more information, contact Word on Fire Catholic
Ministries, PO Box 97330, Washington, DC 20090-7330 or email
contact@wordonfire.org.

First printing, February 2025

ISBN: 978-1-68578-164-4

Library of Congress Control Number: 2024944757

WORDS BY
# THOMAS SALERNO

# THE RIDDLE OF THE TONGUE-STONES

*How Blessed Nicolas Steno Uncovered
the Hidden History of the Earth*

ILLUSTRATIONS BY
## DILLON WHEELOCK

DEDICATION

This book is lovingly dedicated to my mother,
Patricia, who encouraged my insatiable boyhood
enthusiasm for fossils and natural history, and who
always believed I would one day write a book.
Thanks, Mom, for everything.

T.S.

In the year 1666, in the beautiful city of Florence, Italy, the court of Grand Duke Ferdinando II de' Medici saw the arrival of a most unusual object—the partial remains of a great white shark!

Intrepid fishermen had caught the beast off the coast of Tuscany. After a long struggle, they managed to bring the thrashing sea creature onto the beach. Thinking quickly, they tied it to a nearby tree, where they clubbed it to death. They gazed in amazement at the massive carcass— catching a great white (or lamia, as the awesome marine predators were called in those days) was a rare and noteworthy event! When they looked into the shark's cavernous maw they saw rows of wicked-looking serrated teeth as sharp as knives.

WORD STUDY    #001

*Maw*

*The jaws and throat of a carnivorous animal.*

Messengers soon delivered news of the stupendous catch to the palace of the duke. Ferdinando wasted no time in sending his agents to collect it. He wanted his personal team of experts to examine the monstrous fish before it decomposed.

But it soon became obvious that the dead shark was too large and heavy to transport intact. The fishermen hurriedly cut off the head and sent this horrific and smelly cargo to Florence by cart, following the path of the River Arno.

Ferdinando was an enthusiastic student of natural history, and his court was home to a renowned scientific academy. The job of studying the shark head fell to one of the newest academy members—a bookish and modest twenty-eight-year-old anatomist named Nicolas Steno.

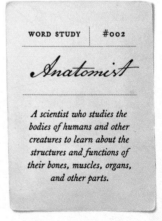

WORD STUDY | #002

*Anatomist*

*A scientist who studies the bodies of humans and other creatures to learn about the structures and functions of their bones, muscles, organs, and other parts.*

Eager to please his noble patron and impress his esteemed colleagues, Steno took to the dissection with his typical fervor and meticulousness. He couldn't have known it at the time, but this moment would forever change his life and the history of science. In the course of his examination,

FIG. 1. Ferdinando II de' Medici

WORD STUDY | #003

*Dissection*

The process of cutting open
a dead animal or plant
to observe and study its
internal structure.

Nicolas Steno would discover a vital clue to a mystery that had stumped learned men for centuries. In his quest to unravel the mystery once and for all, Steno would establish an entirely new field of science and unveil for future generations the hidden history of the world!

Nicolas Steno was born in Denmark in January 1638 to a pious Lutheran family. His parents gave him the name Niels Steensen. But Latin was the common language of scholars at that time, so as an adult he was known to his colleagues by a latinized version of his name—Nicolai Stenonis. In English, he's best known as Nicolas Steno.

An insatiably curious child, young Steno was intensely interested in a wide range of subjects. As a young man, he entered the university at Denmark's capital, Copenhagen, where he decided to study medicine. He hoped to build a successful and distinguished career.

But Steno soon found he couldn't repress his natural inquisitiveness. He studied passionately, learning everything he could about any subject that caught his attention—medicine, chemistry, theology, philosophy, and much more! He devoured all the books he could lay his hands on. His mind was always restless, and he abruptly shifted his focus from one topic to another. He wrote about all of his eclectic interests and passions in a journal he called "Chaos." In it,

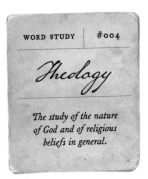

WORD STUDY | #004

*Theology*

The study of the nature of God and of religious beliefs in general.

he copied out lengthy passages from his favorite books word for word.

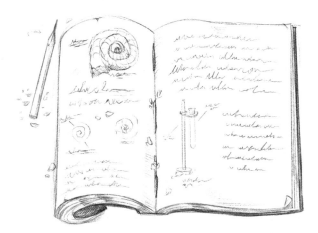

FIG. 2.

Steno's journal

As a student, Steno often worried that his inability to stick with a single academic subject would hurt his career. But it turned out later that his curious, wandering mind was the secret to his success!

After Steno finished his schooling, he made the decision not to pursue the life of a physician. Instead, he began teaching anatomy—the science of how an animal body is put together—and became a master of dissection. Dissection is the practice of carefully examining animal bodies to study their internal structures, such as muscles and organs, nerves and glands.

WORD STUDY | #005

*Physician*

A person such as a doctor, who is medically trained to treat sick or injured patients.

Unlike some other scientists of his time, Steno didn't rely solely on the opinions written down in books by ancient authors. And he didn't leave the bloody and smelly work of dissection to a team of assistants. Steno valued the practice of testing ideas by firsthand observation and experiment.

His skill with a scalpel wowed the audiences who came to the dissecting theater to watch him work. Fellow scholars were impressed by his careful

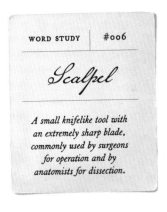

WORD STUDY | #006

*Scalpel*

*A small knifelike tool with an extremely sharp blade, commonly used by surgeons for operation and by anatomists for dissection.*

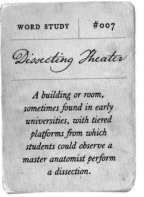

WORD STUDY | #007

*Dissecting Theater*

*A building or room, sometimes found in early universities, with tiered platforms from which students could observe a master anatomist perform a dissection.*

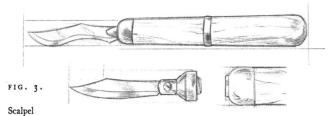

FIG. 3.

Scalpel

observations and by the articulate arguments
he made in the many books he wrote about his
theories.

On one particular afternoon, Steno was dissecting a
sheep's head when he made a surprising discovery.
His metal probing tool revealed an open cavity in
the mouth where the books said none should be.

FIG. 4.

Steno's duct in a
sheep's head

Months later, he repeated the experiment with
a fresh specimen and found the cavity yet again.
He had inadvertently discovered the source of
saliva—the duct for the parotid gland. To this day
it is known to anatomists as "Steno's duct" (or
"Stensen's duct," after a different spelling of his
Danish surname). Accomplishments like this soon
made Steno famous across Europe as an undisputed
expert in anatomy.

Despite his fabulous success in his chosen field,
Steno soon became restless again. He had heard
about the new association of scientists in Florence
called the Accademia del Cimento—the Academy
of Experiment, founded by students of the great
astronomer Galileo Galilei and funded by the
generous support of the grand duke. Excited by
the opportunity to work with the best of the best,
Steno headed over the Alps to Italy.

In Florence, Steno was welcomed kindly by Duke
Ferdinando, and he soon felt right at home. He
was thrilled to be working among a group of such

brilliant and innovative researchers. Like him,
the scholars at the Cimento (pronounced "chee-
MEN-toe") were adherents to the new empirical
method—a system of careful observation and
rigorous experimentation by which scholars worked
to verify or disprove scientific theories.

As a crowd of researchers
and court officials gathered to
watch him dissect the duke's
prized shark specimen, Steno
peered curiously into the great
white's gaping jaws. Steno
was immediately struck by the
predator's triangular, blade-
like teeth. Their shape was
familiar to him—they bore a
striking resemblance to the mysterious fossils called
glossopetrae, or "tongue-stones."

WORD STUDY | #008

*Adherent*

*Someone who believes and
supports a particular set
of ideas.*

Steno had first learned about tongue-stones during
his medical training. In fact, in the seventeenth

FIG. 5. Natural objects believed to possess healing properties

century, physicians were expected to know about all kinds of stones and minerals. For centuries, crystals, gems, ores, and fossils were believed to possess healing properties that could cure a wide array of different illnesses. Tongue-stones in particular were thought to protect against poison, and patients were instructed to wear them as amulets or even ingest them in powdered form!

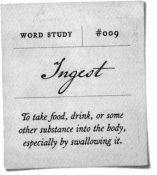

WORD STUDY | #009

*Ingest*

*To take food, drink, or some other substance into the body, especially by swallowing it.*

The origin of tongue-stones and other fossils had puzzled thinkers since ancient times. Fossils that resembled shark teeth and seashells were commonly found in places miles inland and high above sea level, even on mountaintops! How could this be?

WORD STUDY    #010

*Petrify*

To transform the remains of a living creature into stone by the slow natural replacement of its cells and tissue with mineral deposits.

Since fossils bore an uncanny resemblance to the petrified remains of living creatures, some scholars believed that's exactly what they were. But this was not a popular theory, because it didn't seem to explain how shells and shark teeth became embedded in solid rock far from the ocean. Some people speculated that fossils fell from the sky, but the most common opinion was that the strange rocks simply grew in the earth, sprouting up from the

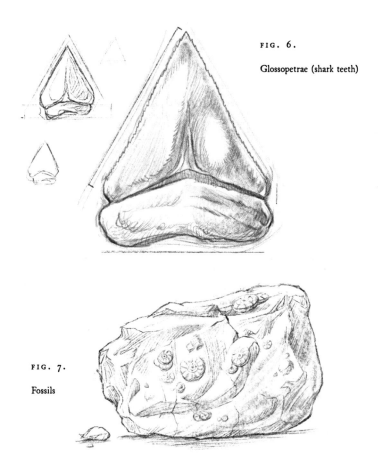

FIG. 6.

Glossopetrae (shark teeth)

FIG. 7.

Fossils

ground like plants. This idea may seem foolish to us today, but in the seventeenth century, scientists were just beginning to understand the power of invisible natural forces, such as magnetism. Who could say what unknown energies were at work in the depths of the Earth? Perhaps one of these invisible forces was responsible for the formation of fossils.

As for himself, Steno was unconvinced by these arguments. After a careful side-by-side comparison of tongue-stones with the teeth of the duke's

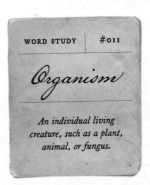

WORD STUDY | #011

*Organism*

*An individual living creature, such as a plant, animal, or fungus.*

great white shark, Steno theorized that fossils were the bones, shells, or teeth of living organisms that had mysteriously turned to stone.

But how was this possible? And how had the fossils of sea creatures come to rest on the tops of mountains?

Steno's unquenchable curiosity and intense concentration became absorbed in solving the riddle of the tongue-stones.

Steno was certain that the Earth itself held the answer. He quickly realized that he couldn't investigate the mystery of fossils unless he could first explain the origins of the rock formations that contained them. To do this, he went out into the field himself to make a firsthand survey of the places where these objects were found. He made extended trips across Tuscany, down to the seashore and up into the mountains, hunting relentlessly for fossils. Steno no longer fretted about his wandering curiosity. Instead, he felt a renewed confidence and a growing sense of purpose.

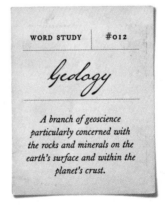

WORD STUDY | #012

*Geology*

A branch of geoscience particularly concerned with the rocks and minerals on the earth's surface and within the planet's crust.

At this time, there were no detailed theories about the origin and history of planet Earth. Geology as we know it did not yet exist. The very idea of documenting prehistory, events that took place long before written records, was unheard of. Almost no one had any clear idea how mountains or valleys or continents were formed. It was assumed that the Earth had remained largely static since the beginning of time. Any changes that had occurred since then were thought to have been caused by chaos and disorder that spoiled God's originally perfect creation.

But when Steno looked at the hills and valleys of Tuscany, he didn't see chaos and ruin at all. His keen anatomist's eye saw how the rock formations and the features of the landscape all fit together in a logical

WORD STUDY | #013

*Static*

The characteristic of being unchanging or inactive.

sequence——a narrative sequence. He saw order: the kind of order that exists in a well-told story!

Steno realized that the Earth's ancient history was written in the ground beneath his feet like the pages of a vast book. But how was one to go about reading and interpreting these pages? Steno needed a framework to decipher the riddles of rocks. He reasoned out just such a framework from his careful observations of the landscape.

Steno noticed that many rock formations were organized into layers, called strata. However, in many places these layers were crazily tilted, folded, faulted, or worn away by erosion. To untangle this confusing jumble, Steno used simple geometry to deduce four brilliant principles to explain the origins and history of rock strata. To this day, if you open up any introductory geology textbook, you can find "Steno's Principles".

WORD STUDY | #014

*Geometry*

A branch of mathematics
especially concerned with
the properties of concepts like
points, lines, and surfaces.

WORD STUDY | #015

*Horizontal*

Level with a flat
surface, rather than at
an angle to it.

WORD STUDY | #016

*Fault*

A fracture across rock strata
along which there have been
significant movements of the
Earth's crust.

# *Steno's Principles*

1. *Superposition*: This word simply means that in any sequence of strata, the layer on the bottom formed first, the next layer formed on top of that, and so on, until the topmost layer, which was deposited last.

2. *Original Horizontality*: This term means that all rock strata were originally formed as horizontal layers, on a roughly flat surface. Later events may cause the layers to become tilted or folded.

3. (A) *Lateral Continuity* and (B) *Cross-Cutting*: When some kind of rift cuts across the strata, it means that this feature formed after the strata formed as continuous layers. (Examples of these rifts include fissures and faults as well as much larger gaps such as valleys or even ocean basins!)

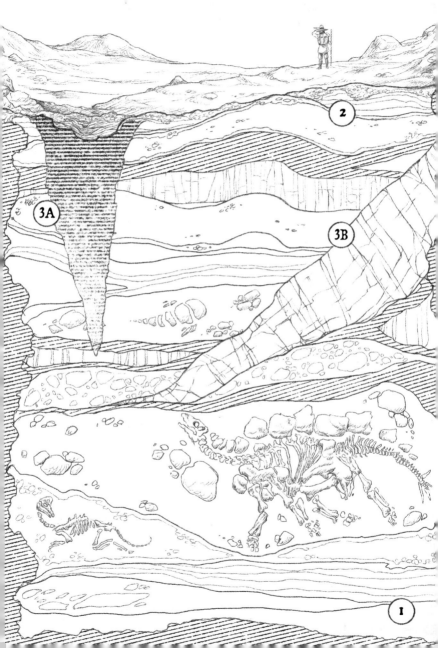

Steno's principles form the basis of the geological discipline of stratigraphy—the study of the arrangement and history of rock formations.

The implications of Steno's ideas were staggering! If layers of solid rock could be older or younger than one another, it meant that the history of the Earth stretched far back into unrecorded time. Thanks to Steno's keen observations and innovative ideas, it is now possible to read the secret history of the rocks and learn about events in the distant past by studying the landscape of the present. Without this fundamental concept, the historical sciences, like geology, could not function.

But how did strata form in the first place, and where did the fossils fit into this new history of the Earth? Steno theorized that fossil-bearing rock formations had actually started out as soft sediment like sand, clay, or mud, suspended in water and laid down over time. He knew from laboratory experiments that larger and heavier grains of gravel

WORD STUDY | #017

*Sediment*

Fine grained matter that is broken down by erosion and often transported by wind or water before being deposited.

WORD STUDY | #018

*Silt*

A loose, fine-grained material carried by running water and laid down as sediment in places like river beds and channels.

and sand sank to the bottom of a glass of water before the finer-grained silts and clays. Steno saw that same pattern of sediment grains in many of the rock formations where he collected abundant fossils.

It became clear to Steno that fossils like the tongue-stones were indeed the remains of

FIG. 8.

Sediment grains in a glass of water as Steno would have observed in experiments

aquatic creatures that had lived in ancient rivers,
lakes, and seas, and which had become buried
in sediment after they died. Over time, as the
sedimentary layers hardened into rock, the durable
parts of these organisms—their bones, shells,
and teeth—were likewise turned to stone: they
were fossilized. The slow, steady work of erosion
eventually brought these fossils back to the surface.

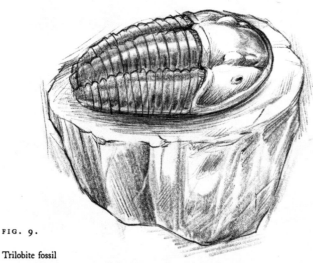

FIG. 9.

Trilobite fossil

Steno wrote up his theories in a brief paper called *De solido*, or "On Solids." But at the same time that he was laying the foundations of an entirely new science, he was also undergoing a profound personal transformation.

Growing up in Denmark, where Lutheranism was the dominant faith, Steno would have been exposed to unfair stereotypes about Catholicism. For example, Protestants often charged that Catholics did not take the authority of the Bible seriously enough. They also sometimes mocked the Catholic belief in the Real Presence of Jesus in the Holy Eucharist as a foolish superstition. But many of Steno's Italian colleagues were Roman Catholics. Their prayerful and virtuous lives inspired Steno. Soon enough, his curious mind began to question the Protestant theology he was taught in his youth.

Steno began to discuss Scripture and theology with his new friends, and he became intrigued by the Catholic claim to be the one true Church founded by Jesus Christ. Steno decided he would not rest

FIG. 10.

Bible

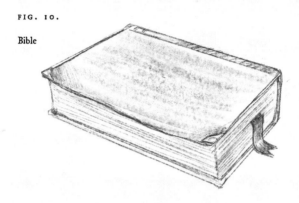

until he had made a thorough investigation of the
question. He pored over the books of the Bible
in their original languages of Hebrew and Greek,
systematically testing the claims of Protestant
and Catholic doctrine against Sacred Scripture.
He brought the same rigor and enthusiasm to his
search for religious truth as he had to his quest to
solve the riddle of the tongue-stones.

While he was pursuing this exhaustive investigation,
Steno witnessed a Corpus Christi procession in
Livorno, Italy. This display of devotion to Christ's

Eucharistic presence was a deeply moving experience for him. Steno found himself strongly attracted to the Catholic faith, yet he was plagued by doubts and hesitant to make a final decision. All that changed one evening in 1667.

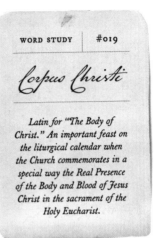

WORD STUDY    #019

*Corpus Christi*

*Latin for "The Body of Christ." An important feast on the liturgical calendar when the Church commemorates in a special way the Real Presence of the Body and Blood of Jesus Christ in the sacrament of the Holy Eucharist.*

WORD STUDY    #020

*All Souls Day*

*The day in the liturgical calendar when the Church remembers the faithful departed and offers prayers for the dead.*

It was the feast of All Souls Day, and Steno was wandering through the darkened byways of Florence seeking the house of an acquaintance. As he stood in the road, momentarily lost, uncertain which direction to take, a friendly voice spoke to him from a window above: "Don't go on the side you are about to go, sir. Go on the other side!"

When Steno heard these simple words, they triggered a deeply personal religious experience. All of his doubts and fears about conversion seemed to fall from him in an instant. Right there in the road he exclaimed with joy, "O Lord, you have broken my chains asunder!" He now felt a deep and serene certainty that his desire to "go on the other side" and convert to Catholicism was the will of God. Steno's restless mind and heart had found peace at last.

Steno finished writing the manuscript of *De solido* in 1668, but he had other pressing matters on his mind. Around the time of his conversion to Catholicism, he received word that the king of Denmark had commanded him to return to Copenhagen to become the royal physician. Steno wasn't enthusiastic about the new job, especially because he didn't think he would be allowed to freely practice his newfound Catholic faith in his Lutheran homeland.

Hoping to bide his time and delay accepting the troublesome appointment, Steno traveled across Europe. Along the way, he continued to practice anatomy, conducting many dissections. But he also spent his time studying the landscapes of the different countries he visited, collecting any interesting minerals or fossils he came across. He had these specimens shipped back to Florence for

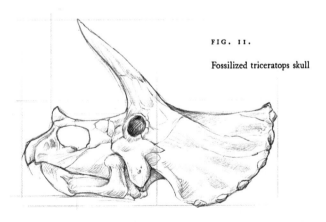

FIG. II.

Fossilized triceratops skull

the grand duke's growing collection of natural curiosities. Steno was on one such collecting expedition in the Austrian Alps when *De solido* was finally published in 1669.

All the while, Steno continued to nourish his Catholic faith, diving deeper into his studies of Scripture and theology. The idea of a deep harmony between the Christian religion and science might seem strange to some people today, but Steno and his colleagues had no trouble understanding that faith and reason are like the two wings that a bird needs in order to fly—they are not opposed to each other but work together in tandem. Most scientists in seventeenth-century Europe were devout Christians who were convinced that all knowledge ultimately has its source in God the Creator. For them, the study of nature was the study of God's handiwork.

After several years of delays and negotiations, Steno finally arrived in Copenhagen to take up

the post of royal physician, and in 1671, he
accepted a professorship in anatomy at Copenhagen
University. But before long, he became dissatisfied
with his situation. He had little time to continue

FIG. 12.

Copenhagen University

his study of fossils, and he found that, as he had suspected, his Catholic beliefs were unwelcome in Denmark.

Steno managed to obtain permission from the king to be released from his appointment. He quickly made plans to return to Florence. He now felt an intense desire to follow Jesus wholeheartedly and discerned that he was being called to devote his life to the service of God and the Church as a priest. No longer wavering or restless, Steno threw himself into his new vocation with his typical fervor and devotion.

The Church soon recognized that Steno's deep scholarly knowledge and his talent for ministry made him an ideal candidate for the priesthood, and he was allowed to skip over the usual period of lengthy theological studies. In 1675, Steno was ordained a priest at the age of thirty-seven. Only two years later he was elevated to the office of bishop! In 1678, he was sent to Germany on a twofold mission: first, to minister to the Catholics who remained in that country after the upheavals of the Protestant Reformation and the Thirty Years' War; and second, to do missionary work evangelizing among the Protestant population.

WORD STUDY | #021

*The Thirty Years' War*

*A series of interconnected wars fought across Europe over three decades from 1618–1648. Millions of soldiers and civilians were killed from battle, famine, and disease during this period.*

Yet Steno had little enthusiasm for the administrative duties of a bishop. Managing the assignments of the clergy and settling disputes among the lay faithful were not among his strengths. All he wanted was to live the simple life of an ordinary priest. But in obedience to the pope, he undertook the German mission. Unfortunately, he did not meet with much success. His first post was in the city of Hanover, but before long, a Lutheran duke came to power there and Steno was forced to leave. He

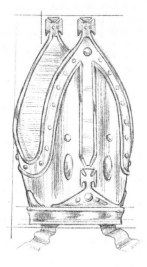

FIG. 13.

A bishop's mitre

arrived in Münster, where he tried to settle down
as an auxiliary bishop. But his uncompromising
stand against corruption in the local Church
and his defense of the poor and powerless soon
made bitter enemies for Steno among his own
congregation. There were some people in his
new diocese who benefited from the unjust
circumstances, and they did not want anyone,

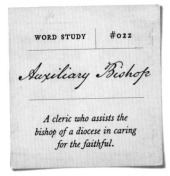

WORD STUDY | #022

*Auxiliary Bishop*

A cleric who assists the
bishop of a diocese in caring
for the faithful.

even a bishop, to interfere with their accumulation of money and influence. Steno was forced onto the road once again. He came to Hamburg, where he took up a simple life of prayer, penance, and poverty.

Steno distributed alms generously. He even sold his bishop's ring and silver crucifix and gave the money to the needy. He took up numerous ascetic practices. He traveled about his diocese on foot, dressed in shabby clothes. He fasted continuously and often slept sitting upright in a chair or lying on a bed of straw on the floor! Steno's demanding life of strict piety

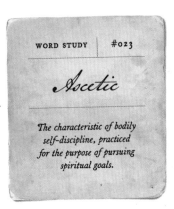

WORD STUDY | #023

*Ascetic*

The characteristic of bodily
self-discipline, practiced
for the purpose of pursuing
spiritual goals.

soon attracted attention, both good and bad. His
friends believed he was a holy man: a living saint.
But just like in Münster, his good example made
him many more enemies, who were scandalized and
offended by his saintly demeanor. Some of these
people even began to send Bishop Steno death
threats!

Steno persevered despite all these setbacks and
frustrations. He even found time to revive his
studies of anatomy. He began taking notes for
a new paper about the nervous system. But the
constant pressure of his many responsibilities was
slowly wearing him down.

Demoralized and weary, Steno wanted to return
to his beloved Florence for a period of rest and
recuperation. But he changed his mind and chose
to stay in Germany when a new opportunity opened
up to serve Catholics in the city of Schwerin, who
were in need of a priest to revive their struggling
community.

This new assignment was to be his last. During his time in Germany, Steno's health had begun to decline. He lost weight and was stricken with chronic discomfort in his stomach. One day, he suddenly collapsed in terrible pain and was carried off to his bed by his staff. In spite of his suffering, Steno managed to write his will and a few final letters to friends and colleagues. As his strength ebbed away, he recited the prayers for the dying in the company of his assembled household. The brilliant scientist and tireless servant of the Church went to his eternal reward on November 25, 1686. He was forty-eight years old.

In Tuscany, the Grand Duke Cosimo III, the son of Steno's friend the late Ferdinando II de' Medici, sent for Steno's body to be returned to Florence and laid to rest in the crypt of the beautiful Basilica of San Lorenzo. His remains have since been moved to a small side chapel called the Capella Stenoniana—Steno's Chapel—where his limestone sarcophagus can be seen today.

FIG. 14.

Rosary beads, a sacramental to help
guide the praying of the Rosary

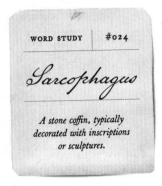

**WORD STUDY** | **#024**

*Sarcophagus*

*A stone coffin, typically decorated with inscriptions or sculptures.*

In 1938, three hundred years after the holy anatomist was born, Pope Pius XI received a delegation of Danish Catholics who petitioned the Holy Father to officially canonize Nicolas Steno as a saint of the Catholic Church. The pope gave his permission for an official investigation into Steno's life and works, and the process of collecting information began soon after in Osnabrück, Germany.

**WORD STUDY** | **#025**

*Canonization*

*A declaration by which the Catholic Church recognizes that a deceased person is a saint in heaven, worthy of public veneration by the Christian faithful.*

Fifty years later, on October 23, 1988, Pope John Paul II presided over Steno's Mass of

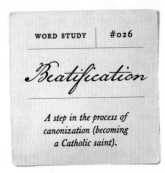

WORD STUDY | #026

*Beatification*

A step in the process of
canonization (becoming
a Catholic saint).

Beatification, declaring
the saintly scientist
"Blessed." Even
though he has yet to
be canonized, Nicolas
Steno is popularly
considered to be the
patron saint of the
geosciences.

Nicolas Steno's scientific
discoveries transformed
our understanding of the
earth underneath our
feet. This humble and
holy genius was the first
to see the outlines of
a secret history written
in the rocks and in the
fossils they contained.

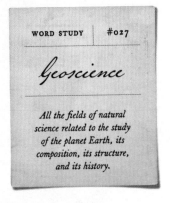

WORD STUDY | #027

*Geoscience*

All the fields of natural
science related to the study
of the planet Earth, its
composition, its structure,
and its history.

His pioneering work on the nature of fossils was
eventually expanded upon by later generations of

researchers. Their theories and discoveries led to the recognition of the new science of geology and laid the groundwork for our current understanding of the primordial history of the Earth, what geologists today often call "Deep Time."

WORD STUDY | #028

*Primordial*

Very ancient, existing at or near in time to the beginning of the world.

In the twenty-first century, geology and paleontology are thriving sciences. The fossil halls

WORD STUDY | #029

*Paleontology*

A branch of the geosciences that reconstructs the history of the Earth and its creatures by studying the fossilized remains of animals and plants.

of natural history museums, filled with the amazing skeletons of long-vanished creatures like dinosaurs, draw millions of enthusiastic visitors from all around the

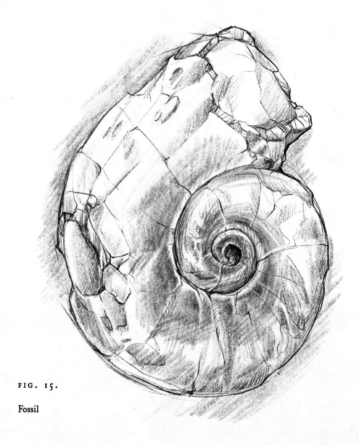

FIG. 15.

Fossil

world. Nicolas Steno and his discoveries made this possible.

And it all began that day in 1666 when the enormous shark head arrived on Steno's dissecting table. It took Nicolas Steno's inquisitive and tenacious mind to discern the hidden connection between shark teeth and tongue-stones and to relentlessly pursue the riddle until he uncovered the answer. God has written his truth in two great books—the Book of Scripture and the Book of Nature. Nicolas Steno had the knowledge and wisdom to read and learn from them both.

# *Glossary*

*Amulet* — A small ornament or piece of jewelry that, according to superstitious belief, can grant the wearer magical protection against evil, disease, or bad luck.

*Anatomy* — The science of how an animal body is put together.

*Cavity* — A natural hollow space found within a solid object such as a human or animal body.

*Duct* — A channel or tubelike structure within a living creature through which flow bodily fluids like tears or saliva.

*Empirical Method* — A type of research that relies on direct observation and experiment to collect data that will either support or undermine a scientific theory.

*Evangelize* — To preach the Gospel, sharing the teachings of Jesus Christ and his message of salvation from sin.

*Meticulousness* — The trait of being extremely careful or precise and showing special attention to small details.

*Saliva* — A watery fluid produced by glands in the mouth that helps with swallowing and digestion.

*Specimen* — An individual object, such as an animal, plant, or mineral, used as an example for scientific research, teaching, or display.

*Stratigraphy* — The study of the arrangement and history of rock formations.

*Thomas Salerno* is an author, freelance writer, and podcaster from Long Island, New York. He has a bachelor of arts in anthropology from Stony Brook University and has also worked in the fossil collections of the American Museum of Natural History. Thomas hopes to inspire young readers to embrace a spirit of curiosity and wonder about the natural world. *The Riddle of the Tongue-Stones* is his first children's book.

*Dillon Wheelock* is an illustrator based out of the Midwest with a focus on the fantastical. He loves fairytales, folklore, and fantasy! He also works in the toy world as a concept artist on both original and established properties. When he's not creating art, you can find him spending time with his lovely wife and son, wandering bookstores, exploring nature, plucking away on the ukulele, or tending to his house plants.